With
A
Broken Heart

Natalie E. Johnson

With A Broken Heart

© 2023 by Natalie E. Johnson

ISBN:9781484871089

Dedication

For those who have navigated the maze of sorrow and emerged stronger, this collection is dedicated to you-warriors of the heart who have weathered the storms of pain and found resilience within the broken pieces. Your strength and courage inspire the verses within these pages.

To the silent sufferers and the brave menders, may these poems be a companion, a solace, and a whisper that resonates with the echoes of your own journey. For every shattered dream, every tear shed in the dark, and every moment of quiet triumph, this collection is a tribute to the invincible spirit that rises, phoenix-like, from the ashes of adversity.

In honor of those who have felt the weight of the world within the chambers of their hearts, "With A Broken Heart" is a testament to the beauty that emerges from pain, the resilience that blooms in adversity, and the healing that comes from embracing the fractures that make us beautifully whole.

With love and empathy,

Natalie E. Johnson

SIGN UP FOR MY AUTHOR
NEWSLETTERS

BE THE FIRST TO LEARN ABOUT
NATALIE E. JOHNSON'S NEW RELEASE
AND RECEIVE EXCLUSIVE CONTENT
FOR BOTH READERS AND WRITERS!

HTTPS://NATALIE-E-JOHNSON.SQUARE.SITE/

ACKNOWLEDGMENTS

I extend my heartfelt gratitude to those whose unwavering support and inspiration have enriched the pages of this poetry collection. Creating this work has been a journey of introspection and creativity, and I am deeply indebted to the following individuals and entities:

My family, for their enduring love and encouragement throughout this creative process. Your belief in my passion has been a constant source of strength and motivation.

My friends, who have been both sounding boards and cheerleaders, offering valuable insights and constructive feedback. Your diverse perspectives have added depth and nuance to these verses.

The lovely Sunni Nykohi for creating the most beautiful book covers for me. You are amazing.

Just What Kind of Love is This?

Just what kind of love is this?
I feel like I'm so alone. No one to share my
feeling with. Why do I feel this way when I
have a man.

Just what kind of love is this?
Maybe because I don't feel the love that I
should be feeling. I give all the love I can just
to not receive the love back. I don't ask for
much just for someone to love me and to be
very true to me.

Just what kind of love is this?
Just to receive nothing, but heartache and to
be heart broken. Why is it so hard to find a
man to just love and cherish you. I thought I
found that someone, but I guess I found
nothing, should I keep looking or stay right
here? Just what kind of love is this?

Love or Hate?

Do I love you or do I hate you?
Sometimes I don't even know all kinds of
stuff keeps running through my head like why
I'm I with you when all you do is make me
feel bad or why haven't I left yet when I still
love you I ask myself is it love or hate? Days I
wish you would just leave and don't come

back those are the days I hate you. Other days I wish you wouldn't leave me alone those are the days I love you. But I ask myself is it love or hate?

Is He All Mine?

Sometimes I sit and wonder is he even mines does he belongs to only me, because when we get in a disagreement he just up and leave. Not knowing where he's at or who have he been with. I just want to know the truth even if it hurts me I've been hurt plenty of time before so this won't be the first and it sure ain't the last Is he all mines or am I sharing him with someone.

I don't know or it could be someone I do know, I don't know, but this question keep running in my mind. What should I think or why am I thinking this? Do I want him to cheat on me or it maybe because of the past men in my life. Is he all mine? Is the question I keep asking myself because something he do make me think that way.

Your Words

Your words are so sweet that you can kill me with kindness. I never met a guy like you saying all the right things at the right time. I enjoy spending every minute with you, your passion for love just drives me insane. Just knowing the right moves and playing the right game.

Your friendship is true that all the ladies would like to have you.

Your words are so painful that it makes me cry, knowing that all this time it was all lies the same guy I love to be with, doing the things that I don't approve of and my feeling to you don't mean shit and it's all because I fell in love with your words.

To My Grand Pa
In the memories of: James Moore

When I was little I remember things you use to drink and smoke, and even cuss us out but that was just you. Grandpa this is for you.

I know you suffered for a long time but now your in a better place and have a piece of mind

Everyone miss you especially me because I didn't say my goodbye to you. I was having problem in my life. I'm sorry grandpa I wasn't there. I hope you forgive me and understand.

Love is What Brought Us Here
In the memories of: Percy Gilbert

Love is what brought us here today. Even thought this is a sad moment Love is always here to stay.
In Gods world love is the key to everything you may never again see the person around you today but if you let them know how you feel that will affect their life in every way, did this man know how you felt?
Well don't be saddened that he didn't know before he passed but he know now who loves him, because God is whispering the roll call that's here today in his ear. I know that you sadden that he passed but rejoice, I say rejoice because no he's not in pain, he's not suffering he's home. Love is what brought us here today even though this is a sad moment love is always here to stay.

Baby It's You (6/8/2004)

Baby it's you that got me where I wanted to be I'm happy when I'm with you now that you took that away what do I have to say. Best friend you were to me Secret lovers we use to be baby its you that love my heart and it was you that also broke it.

I Got Myself Back (7/18/2003)

I have been trapped in a marriage for so long. I became a chameleon that just blended in with whatever was going on. I did as he told me I never complain the things that he did I act like there wasn't wrong in my heart it pound with pain as I got on my knees and asked the Lord to let it rain.

Controlling is what he did best loving me is what he did less. I cry night after night asking for love to come my way when day after day I love you is all he could say.

I got myself back the happy me the lovable me I got myself that's all I need I know it was wrong the way I did it but I seen no other way out of it. I talked with this guy that became my friend he's younger but he was willing to listen to my pain and my problems He help me get through the time that was rough I began to fall in love. I can be myself with him telling him what's on my mind and he would understand and try to help me I got myself back, the happy me, the lovable me I got myself back that's all I need.

My Life Change with A Blink of an Eye
Dedicate to David Walker (1987-2004)

My life change with a blink of an eye My son was taking away from me and I don't know why he went to Ivery Green Village and never came home by a single bullet my David was gone.

My life change with a blink of an eye. I worked hard to put him in a better home never knowing that home would be in heaven now all I want is to talk to him again but the only way he's talking is through his other friends that's the last time he spoke he said I hope you know there's a God. My life change with a blink of an eye

I Love You, I Hate You (12/5/2013)

Today I love you, I want your hands all over me, holding me with yours massaging me, with your hands and kissing me with your lips Baby if I haven't told you yet I'm telling you now. I love you.

Ooo I hate you and sometime I wish you would go away and never return I'm sitting over here trying to clean up the mess you done.

Caught In Your Game (7/10/2000)

Love don't live here anymore not since that night you called me a whore. I never told you we was together as one. I'm just out to have some fun for one your tripping off the wrong thing. When I met you, you had on a wedding ring so tell me what's up with that when we made love you called me Pat, Who is that?, that's not my name sounds to me like you gust got caught in your game.

Trying to play me and you just got played oh by the way you left Pat number on my bed. Yes, I was gonna call her but she called me instead fool I got caller Id before she called my name. I said Hi Pat it's me. Let me tell you before you start he tried to play both of us but in my case that wasn't the part see he just got caught in his game. So what's you going to do now?

Unreplaceable (12/4/2013)
In the memories of Paul Walker 9/12/1973 - 11/30/2013

My heart is broken to find out that you're gone your movies are being watched daily so that your memories lives on. A nice guy you was to everyone that you came in contact with. They spoke of your spirit and your sweet kindness. The fast and the furious will never be the same because there's no one out there that can replace your name.

Men Ain't Shit (10/12/2005)

I could be wrong with what I say but men ain't shit well to me anyway to men men ain't nothing but ass on a stick talking about where they want to put there dicks don't get me wrong but dicks I love its the uff that turn me on Why I said men ain't shit because you some that act like boys and all day long they want to play with there game boy or the X-box when they got a fine woman that want then to hit the spot then you got some that want to be players try to be a pussy slayers then you got some that knows how to treat the woman and you fall in love but you know deep down inside there's wrong because they're fucking married.

You Thought (11/14/2005)

You thought I had to have you in order to breath You thought I needed you by my side. So I could stand.
You thought I couldn't make that decision on my own.
Well it's a lot that you don't know about me see it was me that was and is the back bone

that every relationship needs it was me that been standing by myself while your walking on your knees it was me that took that long deep breath when I let your ass go.

I Can't Give You Me (11/15/2013)

At this moment your asking to much see my heart has been broken with just a simple touch you keep trying to give me something that I'm not even ready for I'm trying to work on me so I ask can you exit my door when I give him my love I want to be able to give him me but right now I can't because I can barely see.

I don't need you to give me your love when I can't give it back. It's not your fault that I'm this way it actually started back in the day, I thought I could handle it by hiding it but I can't hide it anymore. I can't give you me because I'm about to explode I'm not going to put you on this emotional trip that I'm on so let me try to fix me before you come into my world and I promise when I'm done I will be able to be your Queen

Do You (12/5/2013)

Do you see the same person I see when I look in the mirror? Well if you don't let me tell you.

See the person I see is someone who's heart been broken yet she continues to look for love.

Do you see all of her pain? If you understand why this woman welcomes the rain then you will understand it take time to heal.

I'm So Tried (11/25/13)

Today is the day of our wedding but deep down I wish I was dead. I'm so tried of you knocking me upside my head and you punching me in my legs. I'm so tried of making up excuses because I'm the one getting punished and bruised. I'm so tired of being tired and today I refuse to take anymore. So I spoke let me fix your plate as you walked thru the door he smiled and said you shouldn't have in the back of my mind. I'm saying you wish that I wouldn't have after I get finished.
I felt like a winner. See While he was eating I gave him the rest of the hot cheese grits all down his head and some on his chest. The words that he said I dare not repeat as I took his baseball bat to his knee. I told him what was on my mind and told him that this was the last time he was gonna put his hands on me and if he wanted to he could leave. It took everything I had to reach this point but I

had to let him know that I wasn't scared anymore. Tears has fell for the last time someone is going to lose there life and it's not going to be mines.

On A Tight Leash (12/4/2013)
Inspired by the movie N-secure (Robin)

You romanced me with everything from a carriage ride to a glass of champagne. I fell in love with you because you're that man every girl wants there's a secret that no one knows. I'm on a tight leash that only you hold. I try to prove myself to you time and time again. You want to make me your wife but the love I have want let you that far in my life.
You threatening me in a way I don't want to leave. So I do the next best thing I came on to my best friend's man. So alone is how I stand I find out I'm carrying your child now all of a sudden your in denial. We took a paternity test to prove you wrong but paid the nurse off because you knew you was wrong you cut my brakes to take me out you turned me into someone I wasn't about.

Too Little Too Late! (12/4/2013)
Inspired by the movie: N-secure (Jill)
Title Inspired by Errol L. Roberson Jr.

His smile is like a thousand word he place
the ring on my finger for him to be all mines
and I'm all his. You asked me to be your wife
but yet you made out with my best friends
how can you let what we have end.
My heart belong to only you and you
scattered it. How can I look at you after what
you did trying to deal with my broken heart
and trying to decide if I want to take you
back. I got the news that you die in a car
crash. I can't believe my heart been broken
twice. I need to get away cause I loved him
and that second chance neither one of us will
get.

The Heart Breaker (12/4/2013)
Inspired by the movie: N-secure (Tina)
Title inspired by Jermaine Kelly Jr.

When I saw him he was the new brand of
caramel. I patiently waited for his
introduction in detail. He invited me to a
party for him and his wife but by the time I
got there it was a change in his life he's wife
stepped out and some how I stepped in I
went with him on his honeymoon and that's
when we became lovers and friends our

relationship was moving fast but I was enjoying the view when he put that diamond bracelet on my wrist I didn't know what to do saying all the right thins at the right time sending gift at my job and the paperwork I signed. I should have known that he was the jealous type when an old friend stopped to say hi then he pulled out his contract that he wanted me to sign my life over to him accusing me of cheating when all I'm trying to so is love him the moment he grabbed me I should have left but the love for him got the best of me it didn't take long for me to realize that something was wrong with this man how can I be a woman when he won't let me stand. He's tracking me, threaten me, as I try to get away everything he gave me he took away. The at my job he sends bigger gifts and a card that changed my mind about him all because I'm trying to love him. I get a call from his ex she tried to warn me but I jumped down her neck. With a kiss from my neck he changed a slap across my face, I ran trying to get away he came towards me so I cut him with a knife he went down I looked up and there was his ex wife.

Emotional Trip (12/5/13)

I tried to stay by your side but you keep taking me heart for a emotional ride you telling me you love me but telling your boys you can't stand me. Holding me and telling me I'm your world. But then turn around and start kissing that girl.

This trip you got me on I didn't ask for it. So the next stop I'm getting off of it. As of right now you can play that single role because I'm done my heart can't take no more.

The Weather of Pain (4/7/2006)

When the wind blow I hear it telling me it will be ok and he will realize the mistake he made see day after day I wonder what really happen and what went wrong. Because hours after hours my heart keep playing all of those sad love songs.

With drops of pain is the only time I can really cry so that other people won't see the pain in my heart as the tears fall from my eyes. When all hail breaks loose you think we lost our minds but reality you were just wasting our time

That's One Too Many

That's one too many time that I'm going to let your treat me like this coming home when you feel like it and I'm not suppose to get pissed that's one too many time that I'm going to let you put me or caressing me then you need to let me be.

That's one too many time that I'm going to let you bring that girl into my house. I pay the bills so both of y'all can get the fuck out.

That's one too many time that I'm going to let you talk to me that way I'm not one of your bitches so I advise you to watch what you say.

That's one too many time that I'm going to let you leave me with your bad ass kids you helped made them so as there father it time for you to take what you did.

That's one too many time that I'm going to let you act like you don't here what I'm saying once I'll pop a cap in your ass then y'all know that I'm not playing.

Respirator Unplugged (12/05/2013)
Title inspired by: Steven Cleckly

I took my time to smell what I thought was roses but as time went by I realize that the scent I was smelling wasn't of a flower.
It took me a couple of years and over a couple of hours. I noticed that the scent was a scent of your evil spell. Got me saying what

the hell? Because I though I was done receiving your bull consciously lies is what has me full.

I can't breath because of your lies I'm now contaminated. I'm feeling so weak that I have to be elevated. I'm drifting away and you don't even care.

It's your type of love that I have to beware, I thought all this time you was giving me life but slowly you was taking it from me than all of a sudden my respirator was unplugged.

Time For A Change (12/6/2013)
Title inspired by: Adrienne Redd

It's time for a change I'm fed up with your game I stayed in this marriage as long as I could knowing that a long time ago I should have left you, Kicked you out cause faithfulness is what you wasn't about I over looked a lot of things because I was the one that was carrying your name what is it that you carry from me it's not my heart because it's fragile you see and if you knew that you would have been more careful and took better care of it now that I'm gone your missing it. I thought I needed you but I was wrong here's your name back and so long.

I Can't Stop Loving You (3/13/2004)

See Boo you got me trippin I can't stop loving you no matter what you say or do. I'm gonna always be here no matter how you act I got mad love for you and that's a fact. I tried and tried but I just can't stop because I know what we had and I was on top now you're telling me that this relationship won't last. Was it something that was done in the past? Leave it there you have love right here I never once mention that chic that calls. Talking about pick her up from the mall. I can't stop loving loving you.

Bleeding Heart (1/1/2014)

I saw you and I thought you was fine. I wish I could turn back the hands of time. You saw me looking at you so you walked over and asked me how do I do. Before I could say a thing your hand was around my neck like a wedding ring you pushed me down my clothes you tore. You treated me like I was a five dollar whore. The beating I received I don't even know you so why would you compare me.
The tears flow heavily from my face as I'm praying for his mercy and his grace. I opened my eyes just to see who was this person that was raping me and even though I don't know

his face He took from me what can't be replace. My heart bleeds from every angle because in this man's head his mind was tangled. Now I have to deal with this for the rest of my life how can I trust any man better yet how could I be his wife?

My Fault

Life, you didn't have a chance and it was all my fault because of my circumstance. I have been paying for my mistakes for years and when your birth month come around I was depressed bad always in tears.
Never understand why on those months I would cry. As I have been soul searching I know and understand why I felt God was never pleased. I asked for His forgiveness because his love I needed to help me cope with the lost of you two.
I prayed to God to help me name you and when God gave me the names my heart begin to feel better and your names were engraved in a ring. I know that God forgave me and that he was giving me the chance that I should have given you.
I still wonder what you would have looked like and if I keep following God I'll get the right.
I whisper Faith and Jacob, mommy still loves you as I sealed it with tears.

A Touch From A Man (3/26/2004)

A touch from a man, you raised me.
I trusted you never did I think you would do
me like that. Every time the family would
leave in my room you come to touch me.

A touch from a man,
I don't remember when you started but you
always told me that you loved me so I
thought it was ok.

A touch from a man who broke my family a
part I told mommy, it broke her heart.
Daddy, I forgive you for what you done but
never again will I be the one.

By The Hands of Her Lover

By the hands of her lover she would never
tell
I tried to help her but she told me she fell.

By the hands of her lover she was abusc
when questions came about she made an
excuse
that was the first but never the last.

By the hands of her lover wrapped around
her neck.

There's never a witness while they were on
the deck.

By the hands of her lover her life would end
she was very sweet and also my best friend

It's Just Another Day (3/23/2004)

As I enter in the door you call me all kinds of
names. I start to cry because I can't take this
anymore. I work all day and fight all night.
I'm always saying I'm sorry even when I don't
know what I did wrong. I need to get out but
I don't want to be alone. It's just another day.

I try to be nice and do everything your way
but it's the same things every day. We talk,
we kiss and we fight you hit, I duck, and you
miss at times I'm scared to come home
because I know what's going on it's just
another day.

I'm Sorry

Baby, I'm sorry that I did what I did wasn't
thinking about you and reacted like a kid.
Please forgive me and never let me go I do
what I have to until you tell me no. Baby, I'm
sorry really I am I messed up before we
started dam my heart is crying just like your
soul if you leave without trying we will never

be whole. Take this and think about it because it's coming from my heart Michael, I love you and I hope we never part Only God really know where our hearts is at one more rose because I need you back.

Black Eye (03/24/2004)

Black eye, Black eye go away
she gets a black eye every other day
her husband hit and beat on her
she don't know why but out of one eye she
can't see.

Black eye, black eye go away
her family tries to tell her not to stay her
friends tell her to leave him alone but it's
hard to do when he's always home for years
and years she love him and hoping one day
he's change.

Black eye, black eye go away
the beating stops for awhile she found out she
was having his child. She started thinking she
had the answer to the problem so after the
first was born she got pregnant on and on
four kids is what sh had the beating stop she
was glad.

Black eye, black eye go away
he got hipped to the game

his sex he retained

Black eye, Black eye here it goes again
The black eye became her best friend

I'm Accustomed

Why do I keep coming back knowing it's not
worth it.
Is it because I'm accustom to your love? The
beatings, the cussing, also the cheating. I tell
myself time and time again that I'm going to
leave but I keep finding myself at your feet on
my knees pleading for you not to leave.
Is it because I don't want to start over? I
know if I stay one day the dirt they will use to
cover my grave.
I'm accustom to your painful love and you
know that I'm your slave more and more I try
to stand on my own two feet but somehow
your fist and my face always meet and I drop
to my knees. I cry because of the pain you
caused and the sad part is that your a
policeman so you know the laws.

Never Thought

Never thought you would do this to me all the love we share I thought nothing could go wrong but that was a lie from the pit of hell I'm not going to lie I miss you and deep down inside I still love you. But I waited too long for you and for what for you to leave me. I never thought I would be looking for love all over again. Promise you made to me you broke in a heart beat I forgave you and thought this could be you.

Why Do I Feel Like This?

Why do I feel like this? I thought you suppose to feel happy and excited when you found someone you love. Well I don't feel that way I feel like no one can see me I try to please you with everything you want and a little more but you rather take a little and leave the rest at the door.
Why do I feel like this? If you tell me that I'm the only one you need then why do I feel like your cheating on me I've been hurt, and I've been played but this just takes the cake because I'm your slave I do what ever you

ask me to do but when I ask you to do a little something you can't return the favor that I gave you
Why do I feel like this? Alone, Hurt, and Unhappy. I guess because I AM.

Another Man

Can we talk this over? I'm trying to understand you said you don't want to hurt me and you're in love with another man. How can you do this to me after all we been through spending time everyday didn't mean anything to you. How can you love me? When you love the same sex I do you was my lover as well as my best friend now you decided to tell me that this game you were playing needed to end.
How can you play with my heart and bounce it off the wall when all the love I gave, my head I had to fall see you don't understand how I really feel you married me, so the love wasn't really real? I cry tears of sadness never felt joy I was in love with a man that was in love with another boy.

How Do I Know?

How do I know if this time this love is for real? I try not to compare you with the others but that's how I feel. It start off nice and right than it turn up ending all wrong. My love is taking for granted and I'm always singing another one of those sad song about how I mess him and can't live without him. I cry even though I try to be strong but how strong can one heart be when someone always cheating on me.

How do I know if you're not like the rest? You shower me with love then leave me in an empty handed mess I try not to have the same feeling for you as I did my ex because the love I had for his is complex I just want to know how will I know if this is really real because of every lover I had that the same feeling that I feel.

My Heart

My heart is broken and I'm choking, the tightness of my veins.
I can't breathe and I'm crying, cause I'm in pain.
Sitting here in deep thoughts trying to stay cool
my heart took over, now I feel like a fool
smiling in my face while lying to my face
at the same time still trying to invite me to your place
you don't want to commit to a relationship
but want to remain friends with benefits

and I'm asking myself is it worth it
my answer is no
I want to be some one wife not anyone's
whore

Will I Ever Know?

Will I ever know? The way love goes
at time it seem so right but other time it's so
wrong the things that seem to be happening
end up my fault but when love kicks my heart
just hault.
Will I ever know?
The way love works
sometimes I do but it just don't work
I can never please anybody or even satisfied
them either.
Will I ever know?
Or will I always be stuck
Love is so hard to accomplish and so hard to
get over But will I know the way love goes?

Here We Go Again

Here we go again every time I have my heart
mended together someone comes and breaks
it again. All I want is for someone to love me
as I love them But I guess my love is to
strong when my feeling shows something goes
wrong day after day I think that I was the
problem when the only problem I have is

loving you see you can't handle a real woman love your use to that day to day girl some one that you can sex when you want to and tell them what they want to hear but guess what when your ready to settle down and looking for real love the love you issue to me just stop the tape and rewind because this will play again and it's going to mess with your mind like dejavu here we go again all this is turned on you

Broken Heart

The guy I loved I thought he loved me.
I thought I knew him but I guess I don't know anything about him walking around with a broken heart
All the time I thought he loved me he was cheating on me all the time he was making love to me he was really making love to his other lover. I tried giving all my love to him and I gave him every thing he ask for but now I'm walking around with a broken heart. How am I suppose to forget something like this so fast all I hear is oh she'll be alright or she'll get over it. I have real feeling that no one gives a damn about all my life I've been walking around with a broken heart waiting for someone to mend it together.

Lock and Key

My heart is under lock and key because when I fall in love someone decide to hurt me I try so hard to keep my head up thru it all I try to stand up and keep trying but every time I try I keep crying. Looking for my soulmate is hard to find when I think I have him he's not all mine. Come to find out I'm his chic on the side trying to love me but he was just taking me for a ride. My heart is under lock and key until I find the one for me take this how you want it but I'm tried of hurting every time I give a piece of me my heart goes.

It Was You (04/12/2005)

It was you that loved me like a queen that gave me everything a best friend, a lover, and a man you're the one that told me I had to stand. You brighten up my darkest day by letting me know what your heart had to say. I love you deep within my soul. My heart had been fool before.
It was you that hated me like I was your enemy took everything that was into me how can you love me so hard? And hate me so easy what did I do to have you feeling like this? It was you that loved my heart, It was you that also broke it

It Was Too Late (3/24/2004)

It was love at first sight. She walked passed him to see if he might stop to talk to her and like a fish he took the bait. He won her heart with roses everyday and cards Telling her how much he loved her and how much he care.

Slowly all that started to change instead of red roses. She would get black eyes and bloody noses. Two month later she's having his baby the beating slowed up but never stopped. She came home early one day to find cocaine on the desktop trying to put things together on when did he started never found out questions she started to ask it made him mad and he reply with lies It was to late because that night he beat her so bad that she die.

Trust And Believe

Trust: trust is something you took from me now it's going to be hard for another man to complete me what you planted into my mind will be there and when another man comes alone there will always be flashing light of beware. But believe, believe no matter how many times you put me down so I could fall I will continue to get back up and do my best to overcome this pain no matter how many time I stand in the rain

Trust that my love you will never have again the way I loved you wasn't close to the end you choose to be this way so now I have to take this a little further and do it my way. Believe that the pain you put me in I'm getting stronger so I'm going to win In my heart I still have love for you but your friendship I will not do.

I Wonder

I'm laying across the bed wondering if I didn't go through the pain that I have been through would I be here?
Today, what have I learned, have it strengthen me? I can truly say that everyday that I open my eyes and I can see it's a healing process that's planned for me.
I know as I heal I become a new person, a better me see I wonder if I didn't go through the pain will I still be able to heal someone else or say that words because what you went through don't mean that you're not bless see God uses us, the ones that are brokenhearted to get through the others that is not I thank the Lord for using me to bless you and to heal you with my words you are and will be healed and therefore I wonder no more.

Can't Handle Love

I gave you everything kids, my life, my love, my money and my time just to find out at the end you weren't all mine. I fell in love with you and thought I could see but I'm just as blind as blind could be to believe that all the love was giving was by me I caress you as if you were a precious rose so soft but by the time I realize what was going on it was too late because you have found another mate.

What's wrong? You don't like the way I love or you just can't handle it?

Sweet romantic night, slow music, dimmed light, slow dancing, sweet passionate love making that last all night. But to find out those nights don't mean shit to you like it do to me. What's wrong? Can't handle the love that I give. I praise you as if you were a King I don't get any kind of ring that makes us one. Tell me something am I number one or number two because you can't handle the love I'm giving you

It's Just A Crush

When we was in school I had to admit I had a crush but later in life I realize it was just lust. See that night when I thought I was in love with you that's when you broke my heart in two I notice that I was the other girl and that I entered into your **R & B** world.

I was looking for love, and you was looking for a booty call fit now your telling me that I have your heart and it's me you miss. See you don't understand now that we are grown my feeling has changed and I'm moving on how I would of loved to complete your life, have your babies and be your wife but God has a different plan it's not you to be my man.

Beware of A Heartache

I gave you four years of my life. All those empty promise that I'll be your wife. I tried so hard to love you and all I get is the bottom of your shoe. I don't mean anything to you. You never show me you love me or never said I do. Beware of a heartache
I tell you that I'm very much faithful and that is the truth. But that don't mean anything to you. You go run and play like your a single man how can I keep you when I did all I can you get mad at me and start a fight when you know deep down inside that you're not right. Beware of a heartache.
I'm just your maid I do what you ask but that don't mean shit because me ass your future wife I'm just not it. I give you thing that I think that's just a waste of time and money there's never a warning sign until it's too late

of a heartache.

I Don't Want to Hurt Anymore

You would hurt my feeling every chance you get My heart would be filled with pain as my eyes would be filled with tears. I don't want to hurt anymore.
You would call me names even cheat on me, but you never once cared how I felt or what I really mean it took some other person to sweep me off my feet. In order for me not to get hurt by you. I cried and prayed that you wouldn't hurt me again. You resist that feeling and kept hurting me I would give you a chance to make it up to me but you didn't sometimes I thought it was something that I did or said but I didn't. It's something wrong with you leaving you is the best thing I did. I don't want to hurt anymore.

Unmasking The Real You

I trusted you with my friendship and told you things that only you and God knew and when I confronted you, You act like you was brand new your a back stabber and your two-faced. Your friendship I'm replacing. I'm not mad because of course I just found out who mu haters are. It's you that will make me a star.

Tell me why my friendship you mistreated and misused is it because your jealous of my life style or is it because I refuse to follow the steps you take why should I when your friendship is fake. I'm unmaking the real you in your face. I'm quite sure you'll find someone that will take my place so you can befriend them I don't know who they are but I feel sorry for them see I wouldn't put your business out on blast I'm moving towards the future and you are my past.

Kids Mean More Than A Child Support Check

You feel that you don't have to be in his life because I get a child support check every week you don't even call to see if its anything else your son needs.
You would think since this is your only child that you would spoil him rotten, your name is the only name that my son gotten I guess since he gets a Child support check you don't have to check on him. Man up and take your place because your son would love to see your face spend time with him teaching him things that a father would not letting any other man do what you should see my child means more than a check to me.
As a mother I take care of him and try to nurture him to see his every needs are met,

trying to teach him to be the man that you're not. I love him with all the love I got it hurts my heart everyday because when I look at him I see you our son is more than a child support check.
With God's help God allow him to be in our life not just mine. I shouldn't be the to pick up the phone every time. Man up and be the father that your father was not. Change the generation because this has to stop your child is more than a child support check.

How Come

Why do I have to be second how come I can't be first? You're the one calling me to quench your thirst. When you need someone to talk to and comfort you. I was right there. When you needed good loving my legs are spreaded in the air. This is something I can't understand you talking about need a good woman when you can't even be a real man.
How come I can't be first all the hours I put in I can call it work. You now bringing up that you got a wife I don't give a dam about your other life like they said what happen in the dark shall come to the light. How in the hell you got a wife when it me your with every night? How come I can't be first why are playing games trying to take all my goodies and pulling my chain you must forgot who

you're dealing with I'm Ms. Sensual not your average chic.

Deeper Than A Heartbreak

I can't believe you did me like this knowing my past pain. My best friend is the rain or the water from the shower head. I'm trying to stand but you keep pulling me down instead of loving me, helping me become a better me. I try not to bring the anger from the last man that wouldn't let me stand but it's hard to do when I see the same pattern in you but the pain you caused me is a lot worst and I know this healing process has to take it course even though you are out of my life you have my daughter wanting to be your wife this pain is deeper than a heartbreak.

My heart is starving from the lack of love because I have more than a heart ache, I'm starting to hate the way you guys treat us and you wonder why these women are bitter and always fussing

Still Searching (4/6/2005)

I'm still searching for my King to met up with me. My heart and my soul is in need for that guy to love me just right for his hand to be is my hand as he spend the night making love under a candle that's lit every night the mood

is right but there no man here feel me.
I'm still searching for my King here. So I can cook up a soul food dinner than I won't be still searching, When he don't have to worry about making love cause I'll be right there. I'm still searching for my King because deep down inside I'm ready to be his Queen!!

Missing You

It's been a year since I last saw you, you call me every three days and the question you always ask is how are you doing and with the same answer I reply missing you.
I write you everyday because I have so much to say how much I miss you and I need you to come home. You never met the child we made together it gets harder every day when your not here because your son looks just like you I try not to be sad when I look at him but I'm also happy when I look at your son because I see you in his eyes wishing that you come home. I'm missing you.

I'm Not That Chic

I dropped you the moment you started treating me like a side chic. I'm worth more than what you offering what made you think that that's my position. When we first met wasn't you listening. I gave you more then I planned because you had my heart and you wasn't even my man. See some chics are cool with it. I need love not just a piece a dick my body you took for granted boy you got me twisted and slanted.

I have a heart so stop trying to abuse it you leaving me messages cause I no longer taking your call look how many times I'm going to tell you I'm more than a booty call. Baby I miss you and I love what you give me isn't that the line that you said Dude I don't need your money and I'm staying out your bed if you love what I do than that sound like a wedding bells but since I know that it's not going to happen here's a one way ticket to hell.

Broken Trust

You don't even know the pain that I been through you don't even realize that I was molested when I was nine and with that I have broken trust.

So how can I trust you when you tell me how you feel. When the person that I fell for broken me, broken me to the point where I trust less and I try to do me more, but I also understand that do me more only hurts me because I don't know the true meaning of love and when I say that I love you deep down inside I feel like I do. But how can I love if I don't trust and how can I trust if I love and how can I even make anything when I keep breaking everything and how can I break everything when I don't have anything.

Just a lonely broken vessels, a vessel that needs mending and mending me is going to take a whole lot of work. You know that cherishing me and nourishing me reading me. Trust me enough to let you know that I don't trust and if I see the same pattern that I seen in the last man I automatically think that you have used me and abuse me and a tear shed and my head falls with my head falling down and my tears fills my eyes I'm now disappointed because I spend all my time and all my love trying to express to you. Trying to gain that trust but every tome I trust someone they abuse me, they use me, they mistreat me, and don't guide me.

So now I'm here again all alone. Don't know who to turn to and I can't even pick up the freaking phone because the person I need to talk to don't even have a dial tone. So I get on my knees and pray.

Lord please help me be able to trust again, guide me and strengthen me through all that I have been through and all of my sins see they don't even realize that my pain started when I was nine and when I was nine I was molested, you don't even know by who and you already judging. See most people don't realize and don't understand that you can get molested by a female as well as a man and in my situation it was my best friend.

When I was nine she was twelve and I didn't understand but as I grew up and I wrote my first novel that was the only therapy that I had so with all these years gone by and not having someone to talk to about my pain, that pain grew then it went from me being molested to being abused by my first baby daddy and I wasn't even with him then from there it went to my first husband when he burned me with the iron and guys cheating on me left and right and I don't even know where to stand anymore.

When I say that I have been through the pain I have been through it all you know I can't even recall when it all started but I do know that I'm broken-hearted and I don't even know when my heart would mend because I don't trust and if I don't trust how can I love and I know in the Bible it tells me to do those things and I'm trying, and I'm trying, and I'm trying, and I'm trying, and I'm trying, and I'm trying and I can't and tears just continue to fall and I don't know I don't even know y'all and I know its time for me to do this because I know that I'm not alone but it feel like I am so I close with a prayer Lord please I'm asking you, I'm begging you mend my heart, make me trust, let me love let me be you.

I Was There

I was there with you when you didn't have nothing I told you be patience and your time will come you went from a one bedroom apartment to a four bedroom home. I knew one day you would come out of your trial and struggle.
I was there with you when you needed to cry asking question that I couldn't answer but I was always by your side loving you when you needed to be love listening to you when you needed someone to talk to. I knew one day you would come out of your trials and struggle.
I was there with you when you went form job to jobless. I never gave up or doubted you because I knew deep down inside your doing the best you can do. I knew one day you would come out of your trails and struggle.
I was there with you when you had nothing but a pad and a pen promising me that one day your struggle would end.
I was there kissing every tear that fell from your face I was there to help you run that race.

How Are We Suppose To Have

How are we suppose to have a relationship when you keep telling me them lies. Telling me that you over your brother house when your with that girl on the other side you got the wrong girl to play that game. I'm only going to let you play for so long before I act insane. I will cut up your clothes and your tires too. Don't ask where your jewerly because I pawned them too.

How are we suppose to have a relationship when you saying your out of town when your really around the block. All this bull shit is gonna stop. Those I love you baby and your the only one is getting really old and your shit is over done.

How are we suppose to have a relationship and what make you think it's gonna last I can't even trust you for the shit you did in the past.

It's All Good

It's all good but hell I should have known that it was someone else when you didn't bring your ass home. What type of woman are you looking for because I guess I'm not it. I come home from a ten hour job to cooking you dinner and keeping the house clean. I'm not your dam n maid if you think that's what the word wife means.

It's all good that you show your face every now and then because while fucking someone girl I could be fucking your friend but hell you'll never find out. I'm not complaining cause your paying the bills but I fell in love with you not what's in your pocket or your pants.

You Don't Amount To Anything

You told me that I wouldn't amount to anything see those words has me in a boxing ring and I am swinging like I'm Lala Ali and bitting and spitting words like Mike Tyson because I refuse to be what you said I would be and that is not to amount to anything see when I reach the top I will see you there rather it's there with me or me looking down at you but I refuse to take those words that you said that I wouldn't amount to anything.

See I'm going to express to you what those words really mean to some people that's just a boost of energy others well you know they will fall in your trap and they don't know how to get back but I'm going to let you know today that I'm here standing not because of what other say but because of the words you said because you didn't believe in me now I'm standing on the top. Own my own business and publishing books of three and I'm not going to stop there I'm going to keep going because of the God Almighty oh how I love when I hear the words you're not going to amount to anything that's just like me and him wearing a wedding ring those word are going to stick with me forever not to bring me down but to just boost me you knew that those words was just like striking a match and buring my feet you knew that those words that I need to get me to where I'm at in life but those word you can't uses on everybody because everybody isn't me you won't amount to anything is just a stepping stone and I will contiune to sept higher and higher and higher and higher and I aspect you to be standing right there beside me to doing the exact some thing do I need to say the exact same words to you that you said to me to put the fire under your feet look you don't amount to anything now take those words and put them in the ring

Why You Picked This Day

Why you picked this day to put me out. It's our 18th Anniversary to start screaming and shouting. I did everything for you I even put your broken ass in school now you trying to play me like I'm some uneducated fool. I helped you get to the top now that you're there it's me you want to drop.

I knew what you was doing your secret you couldn't hide from me. Yes, I knew you was cheating on me. My heart told me to give you a chance to prove to me that you were a man you wanted kids that I couldn't give you how would you like it if I did that same to you. Why you picked this day to show your ass in front of this chick.

Fear   (5/14/2014)

What are your fears? Something you refuse to do or have you in tears. I know that I'm not alone in this but I realize that even though it's seem small we have to face our fears not some of them but we have to face them all.
Satan placed in us fear because he knows that the only way he can stop us to succccdn I myself have fears of riding by semi-trucks and I have fears of height but what's the real reason why I'm scared of these things and deep down. I realize my real fear is death but see that's just part of the problem so I'm going to break it down so we can all can solve them because if your scared to die your really

saying that you are afraid to live and if your scared to love your really saying that you're afraid to express your feelings.

And being a poet and poetress that's what we do so what is it that you're really afraid of? We don't realize how serious this is or could be I hope with this I put some deep thought within your soul. So that we can become a better person.

His Disease (12/08/2013)

All I asked was for him to love me
but he could not stay faithful to me
See he had to have Susan and Kim and Kerri
and now the disease he gave I'm carrying
I never asked for this just only his heart
now for the rest of my life I have to live with
this disease and with this disease no one else
will want me.
So my heart stays lonely and my soul is
crushed because of his love that I wanted so
much
he could not be faithful and with him not
being faithful that gave me what I have I no
longer have a piece of mind or a pumping
heart cause every second of the day that pass
is a dying moment for me and it's all because
of his disease.
My family now moans at my body that lies in
this casket I didn't ask for this! No!, I didn't

ask of it. But because of him I'm here and where is he now if you look over he's right next to me.

It's Not Over (03/27/2004)

You up and left me with no excuse my love for you was never a mistake now you came back to get married. The love we have never ended it just stopped it was because of you It's not over.

Our love is still strong. One kiss from my lips still turns you on, your knees get weak and your eyes get glossy it's not over.

Your mouth say one thing but your heart says something different you still look at me as you did when we first met. The way we made love you'll never forget the woman your marrying she's not for you you said that we was forever but your words wasn't true that woman is not telling you what you need to know that your not the only man in her life what we have baby it's not over.

Don't Have Time To Cry

My heart is broken deep down I'm choking because my soul you hold tight you tell me that it's not you that I need yet it's me that you call to spend the night to sex you like I belong to you but yet you said I'm not the girl for you. Now I'm here today trying so hard to make the pain fly I sit at work day dreaming because I don't have time a cry.

Trying to find things to do so I won't think about the pain how I wish today's forecast would call for rain so I could stand in the middle of the grass to let all this pain go away but a part of me saying he's not worth my tears so how am I suppose to let go of this pain. If I don't have time to cry. I keep life morning and take this as a tool to learn. But I don't want the next guy to feel the heat because of my heart he burned

From The Two People I Love (12/29/2005)

From the two people I loved the most. My marriage was ruined and my friendship was a host. I never though that this could happen to me from the two people I love so deeply. My husband told me he love me and I thought it was true until I found out he's deeply in love with you. He tells me every day how he need you in his life but why did he make me his wife?

See I know how strong his feeling are for you the only way to hurt him is to keep him away from you and you had the nerves to tell me that you're in love with my husband, but yet you keep it a secret until we got married now you telling me it's child your carrying because I couldn't give him one from the two people I love my life is done.

SPECIAL COUPON FOR YOU

Thank you for ordering my books the next book is on us with FREE SHIPPING. Get Free Shipping when you enter this coupon code.

Coupon Code :

FREESHIPPING

More Info :

https://natalie-e-johnson.square.site

I hope you enjoyed reading this book of poetry as much as I enjoyed writing it. So if I can ask for your feedback and support it will help me to improve my future writing projects. You can leave a review on my Facebook page @natalieejohnson23 as well as an Amazon review.

Thank you so much for reading this book and I hope you will check out my other work that is coming soon.

Other Books by Natalie E. Johnson

In The Dark
Within The Heart Of Love
In The Memory Of Trayvon Martin
A Touch From A Man (Novel)
Married Without A Groom
At Your Service (Novel)

Natalie E. Johnson also have created Journals and Notebooks

Upcoming Books by Natalie E. Johnson
These books aren't in order:

With A Broken Heart (Poetry)
Within Erotic Treats (Poetry)
Within My Spiritual Soul (Poetry)
Erotically Loved (Poetry)
In Between Happiness (Novel)
A Best Friend's Secret (Novel)
Got To Get My Feet Wet (Novel)
Yo Grind Is My Grind (Novel)
Having Coffee With God (Novel)
My Christmas Romance (Novel)
Leave Your Clothes On The Floor (Novel)
I Wish I Could have This Moment For Life
(Novel)

ABOUT THE AUTHOR

Natalie E. Johnson, a multifaceted creator and storyteller, is not only a mother of five and a grandmother of five but also the proud owner of Natalie's Cleaning Service, a business she has successfully nurtured for seven years. Born with an innate passion for words, Natalie's journey as a writer began at an early age, laying the foundation for a literary career that would later captivate readers worldwide.

Although she started crafting stories in her your, it wasn't until 2013 that Natalie took the courageous step of sharing her creations with the world. This marked the beginning of a prolific writing career that has seen her receive numerous accolades for her poetic prowess. Her ability to articulate emotions through verse has garnered widespread recognition, including the prestigious Editor's Choice Award from poetry for four consecutive years (2003-2006).

Natalie's poetic achievements extend beyond digital recognition with her poems "When," "A Touch From A Man," and "His Disease" earning her the Certificate of Excellence and an Honorable Mention in the esteemed collection "Great Poems of The Western World." Her work was also featured in the anthology "Expression," further solidifying her status as a distinguished contemporary poet.

One of the most poignant chapters in Natalie's creative journey emerged from a deeply personal experience. Molested at the age of nine, she found the courage to share her story through the medium of poetry. The resulting poem. "A Touch From A Man," not only became a powerful confessional but also inspired her to transform it into her first novel, a significant milestone she celebrated by publishing it on her birthday in 2017.

Beyond her literary pursuits, Natalie finds joy in spending quality time with her family, engaging in various crafting endeavors, and undertaking DIY projects. However, it is her passion for writing that remains the driving force in her life. She discovered this passion later in life but has since embraced it wholeheartedly, with gratitude for the divine intervention that led her back to her pen.

As an award-winning poet and author, Natalie E. Johnson continues to inspire and connect with regrades through her evocative words. Her life story, marked by resilience, creativity, and a commitment to authenticity, serves as a testament to the transformative power of storytelling. Each piece of her work reflects not only a journey of personal healing but also an invitation for others to find strength and connection in the shared human experience.